TRAVEL SECURITY

Personal Travel & Vehicle Security

Orlando Wilson

D1730720

To develop a full knowledge of personal security and close protection this book should be read in conjunction with Orlando Wilson's other books on counter terrorism, travel security, home and office security, kidnap and ransom, self-defense and working in hostile environments.

Cover designed by Orlando Wilson

Orlando Wilson
Visit my website at www.risks-incorporated.com

ISBN-9781980702405

CONTENTS

Introduction

These days when traveling internationally you must take into consideration your personal security with that of family members and associates traveling with you. Before you travel anywhere you should take time to research where you are going and work out some basic security procedures and discuss them with those traveling with you.

Before you travel ensure that all your passports and required visas are in order, even slight discrepancies can lead to long delays when passing through immigration and customs. Make sure you are not taking food items that are prohibited to take into that country, most countries immigration and customs departments websites list items that are prohibited. If you are traveling with medications make sure they are properly labeled and check to ensure your medical insurance will be valid in the countries, you'll visit.

Have a pre-arranged car to transport you from the airport to your hotel, most quality hotels can arrange this for you. At busy times taxi queues can be chaotic, there is also the problem of the taxi drivers not know your hotels location and over charging you.

Always check in detail the hotel that you will be staying at, these days a simple web search can pull up customer reviews, always check the reviews on several different websites. Have some security plans for you stay in the hotel, ensure everyone knows where for fire exits are, always put valuables in the room safe when you are out and never to let strangers into your rooms. If an unannounced member of the hotel staff wants to enter your room always call the hotel reception to confirm their identity.

You need to be aware of any political protests or rallies that may be occurring around your hotel or locations you will be visiting. You can do this by checking the local media and talking with the hotel staff. It is best to avoid all areas where political protests or rallies are taking place. Many start out with a carnival atmosphere and can quickly turn in to very hostile situations.

It is sad they we need to discuss this, but you have a plan for want to do in the case of a terrorist incident, I cover dealing with terrorist attacks in my book "Counter Terrorism: IED/Bomb & Active Shooter Response". Make sure you have the contact details for your local Embassy and have funds available for if you must extend you stay due to say an incident at your departing airport.

In most major cities and tourist locations the police are used to dealing with people from all social and cultural backgrounds; a lot of the police officers themselves will be from diverse cultural backgrounds. If you are victim of a crime in U.S. or Western Europe you should always report this to the police, quality hotels will always assist you with contacting the police and most major police departments have interpreters on call if you do speak the local language. When dealing with the police always remain calm and polite, especially if you are involved in a misunderstanding or an incident.

If you follow these very basic guidelines and the more detailed information in this book, you should be able to travel safely in most locations.

Safe Travels,

Orlando Wilson
Risks Incorporated

International Travel Security

You should compile a threat assessment on any area, city or country that you are visiting be it for business or pleasure. These days with the internet it's easy to find crime rates and reports on nearly all countries and areas within them. With Google Earth and the like, you can get high quality aerial photos and street views on most places, which can be used to check out hotels, locations to be visited and select routes.

If possible, send an advance person or team or get a trusted local to check things out and plan for you visit. If you are traveling in a group, consider sending a member or two ahead a few days in advance to check things out and plan before the main body of the group arrives. Below is a basic list of things that you will need to consider before traveling.

- Compile threat assessments on hotels and locations to be visited?
- Will you need any inoculations against diseases or need to take preventative medication with you?
- Do you have trusted contacts at this location and how can they assist you?
- If you're traveling internationally do need visas to enter the country?
- Where will you be staying?
- Can you carry weapons, will you need permits and where will you be getting the weapons from?
- What restrictions are there on carrying weapons and what are the local laws on use of force?
- Will anyone meet you at the destination airport, if yes, do you know them. If not get a photo and arrange code words?
- Will your phones work at the destination, if not where can you get a local mobile/cell phone? What international dialing codes are you going to need?
- Are there payphones at the airport and do they take coins or credit cards?
- How will you get from the airport to your hotel?
- Will baggage be secure and who will have access to it?

- Are you taking local currency with you or are you going to need to change hard currency?
- Will there be ATM's available and can you use your bank cards?
- Will you be able to use credit cards?
- Will you have internet access and is it secure, are there free hotspots?
- What standard of medical facilities are available at the destination and will you need to take sterile or emergency equipment with you?
- Will you need to take prescription medication with you and are there any restrictions on it within the country your visiting?
- Is clean blood available in hospitals at the destination, if not where is the nearest source or clean or synthetic blood?
- Is medical insurance needed and is what you have recognized, or do you need hard currency for ambulance services and treatments etc.?
- Know the locations of hospitals or reliable doctors in your area that can treat trauma or any medical condition you or your fellow travelers may have?
- What are the details of backup hotels and locations that can be used as safe houses or emergency rendezvous points?
- Do you or any of those traveling with you have any special dietary requirements or allergies?
- Is the tap water drinkable or will you need bottled water, if yes is it readably available?
- How will you be traveling around; public transport, on foot or using a driver?
- If you are renting a car make sure you know your routes, have a reliable break down plan and spare tire etc. in the vehicle.
- When driving around make sure you know where the nearest gas stations and emergency facilities, such as hospitals and possible safe locations.
- Who locally knows your program, try to keep things on a need to know basis.
- Make sure someone trusted knows your program and can alert authorities if there are any problems.
- Arrange to make coded check calls to a trusted people within and outside of the country. Select words that can be inserted into a phone call that can mean things are OK or they have gone bad.
- Put together contingency plans to cover any possible crisis be it kidnapping or a serious car crash.
- Have several alternative planned routes by which to leave the country.

- Always keep you travel papers and a reasonable amount of cash hidden on your person that can be used in the case of an emergency where it might not be possible or a sensible option for you to return to your hotel.

This is just a list of considerations that will hopefully get you thinking and help you put together plans and procedures for any future trips you'll be taking.

Adventure Travel & Deployment Kit List

I am always being asked advice about what equipment should be taken on trips to out the way places. My initial response is take as little as possible, more you know, the less you need right! With the below items you should be able to operate for extended periods of time. The below items should fit into a medium size day sack that should be able to carry onto a plane. Items like pocket knives etc. would need to go checked or found at location. This is a guide and not all these items will be required on all trips, do you threat assessments and plan all trips properly before you travel.

Personal Kit

- $500.00 USD minimum in cash, small bills, to be split up, water proofed and concealed in various locations on your person. Same for credit and bank cards.
- Communications, will cell phones work, can you get local phones/chips. Remember chargers!
- Day sack and fanny pack/belt pouch
- Watch
- Pocket knife & multi-tool (unable to take as carry-on luggage)
- Personal first aid kit: tampons, gauze, duct tape, bobby/safety pins and an anti-septic cream.
- Water bottles + purification tabs (water can be boiled in alloy bottles!)
- Bug juice + sun block
- Maps (water proofed) and compass
- At least one Flashlight + spare batteries
- Lighter
- Personal water filter
- Bogota lock picks, lock shims & diamond/needle files
- Para cord
- Duct tape

- Wash kit: tooth brush + paste, soap, razor
- Sewing kit
- Smoke signals + flares (unable to take as carry-on luggage)
- Blanket (poncho liner)
- Poncho (for shelter and use as a rain coat)
- Note book and pens and post-it notes
- Laptop
- Camera/Video
- Emergency power, batteries or solar etc.
- 2 X extra pants (quick drying) and long sleeve t-shirts (under-armor type, Wal-Mart brand works, consider colors, do you want to be seen or not!)
- At least 2 X pairs of extra socks
- Boots (broken-in), flip-flops
- Gloves and Balaclava (if tactical)
- Weapons if legal and required
- Local laws on use of force

Additional Considerations
- Sources of food and water
- Accommodation and electricity
- Laundry service
- Where can you change currency?
- Additional operational equipment

Emergency Vehicle Kit
- Gas containers
- Tube to siphon gas
- Fix-a-Flat X 2 and/or tire plugs
- Tire plug kit
- Portable air compressor (Tire inflator)
- Jump leads
- Tow rope

How Criminals Operate

You need to be aware of how criminals and terrorists operate and what they look for in their victims; if you know this, you can hopefully avoid becoming a victim yourself. Criminals and terrorists are generally business people; they commit crimes to make money or achieve a goal- some are good at it and some are not. At all levels of the crime business, criminals, to some degree, plan and organize their jobs, whether it is stealing someone's watch or assassinating someone.

In this chapter we will refer to the bad guys as criminals and will not differentiate between criminals and terrorist, they are the same. You must remember that terrorists largely fund their terror campaigns from the proceeds of crime be it street crime, providing protection for criminal groups, smuggling drugs/people, protection rackets, kidnapping etc.

I tell my clients that the three golden rules to personal security are think like a criminal, keep a low profile and always have an escape route.

- **Think like a criminal:** Put yourself in the criminal's shoes and think how you would rob or kidnap yourself, how would you break into your home or hotel room.
- **Keep a low profile:** Do not draw attention to yourself, consider what you wear and drive, don't be loud and rowdy. And don't tell strangers to much about yourself, especially anything to do with your personal security. If you are trying to impress someone use a cover story.
- **Always have an escape route:** Make sure you know how and have the means to get out of your location to a safe area. Know how to get out of the hotel and have the means to get out of the city, then possibly the country and you know how to get to a safe location.

Be assured there is nothing listed here that criminals don't already know.

Street Crime

In general, the type of criminal most people will encounter will be from the lower echelon of the criminal world, such as muggers, car thieves, burglars and other petty criminals.

Think about if you were a mugger and you were going to rob yourself what three questions would you ask yourself about the target. Muggers will generally ask themselves three questions when choosing their victims: do they have valuables on them worth taking, will the target put up a fight and can they escape after committing the crime? The criminal has just done a basic threat assessment.

Wherever you go, you need to blend in with the environment and the people around you, so don't make a common mistake and wear expensive jewelry or clothing. Look online for some photos of street scenes from the location you'll be visiting and see how people dress.

It also makes sense that if you are dressed to blend in with your environment, so your luggage should blend in as well. If you are a criminal taxi driver at an airport looking for targets for an express kidnapping who will you want to pick up, the local with the sports bag or the foreigner in the tweed sports coat with the designer leather luggage.

Luggage theft is also big business, in the early 1990's there were crews of Latin American's who use to go to London during the summers and just steal luggage from the lobbies of 5-star hotels. Think what valuables people keep in their suit cases; jewelry, computers, cameras designer clothes etc. Whenever you check into a hotel keep your luggage with you and look around at others luggage and see how easy it would be to walk away with.

Luggage security is also something most do not consider, but consider this; you arrive at your hotel in a developing country and let the bell boy take your bags to your room for you while you complete your check in. You then proceed to your room and start to unpack, then there is a knock on your door. When you answer it there is the hotel manager and two police officers who ask to search your room, are you going to say no, can you say no? When they search your bags they find a small package of drugs, now are you going to pay the fine or go to a 3rd world prison? Do you think anyone will believe the drugs were not yours; there are 3 witnesses who were present when they were found in your bags. Never leave luggage unattended, in some places you need to be more concerned about things being put in your bags rather than taken!

If you are traveling to another country, it makes a lot sense not to advertise the fact that you are foreigner. There are many police forces that supplement their salaries by stopping and shaking down foreign visitors. In the late 90's I had an associate go to Moscow with a client who was dressed as he would in London, camelhair overcoat etc. The Moscow polices spotted him and called over and asked for his wallet, they took $100.00 and gave him his wallet back. A simple a painless lesion, which I hope, but doubt he learned from.

Another way to signal that you are a foreigner- and a potential target- is the language you speak on the streets. If you are in a high crime area and don't speak the local language, try not to talk whilst on the streets and if you must, keep it low. Criminals always look for people who are soft targets because they don't want a confrontation, thus drawing attention, which is bad for business. You always want to act like you know where you are going and what you are doing and not to look and act like a victim.

When traveling, it is important that you plan your trip in detail from start to finish. For example, when planning the trip from the airport to your hotel, make sure that you use a reputable taxi company, such as one which is recommended or supplied by the hotel. Then, when being picked up make sure to verify it is the real taxi that has been sent by the hotel. Airports such as Simon Bolivar Airport in Caracas, Venezuela are very dangerous places and the starting point for many express kidnappings.

Think about it: would you let close family members or friends get into a car with a stranger where you live now? So, why does it in a foreign country, carrying a suitcase full of valuables? In many countries, the taxi business is unregulated and often associated with criminal activity- taxi fares are a source of hard cash and if someone can drive, they are qualified to be cab drivers. Licenses can be bought or copied. The taxi business is also a good corporate front for organized criminal groups as it is a cash business and can be used for laundering Narco money and the like.

Many tourists have found themselves left on the side of the road, in the middle of nowhere watching their luggage, passport and traveler's checks being driven off into the night. The lucky ones just get robbed and not raped, beaten senseless or murdered.

You should make sure you are staying in a reputable hotel that has good CCTV and professional 24-hour security personnel (we will cover this more in depth in a later chapter). You also want to make sure that the restaurants, clubs and bars you go to are reputable. Criminals like to go to restaurants or other tourist hangouts just as much as everyone else. In some places organized criminals are the only ones with the money to set up and frequent upscale restaurants and clubs. Incidentally, criminal venues can be very peaceful places to go but there is always the potential for problems and are therefore best avoided. Criminals will pay waiters or bar staff to tip them off when a suitable victim is noticed at their venue; the foreigner with the Rolex, designer cloths and the wallet full of cash and credit cards. When the victim leaves the venue, they can be robbed on the street or steered into a criminal taxi.

You also need to be careful that when you are in a club or a bar you do not leave your drink unattended. Think about how many times when you have been at a hotel bar or club and left your drink unattended or with someone you have just met who seemed like a nice person. How easy would it have been for someone to spike you drink with drugs such as Rohypnol/Flunitrazepam. This commonly thought of as the "Date Rape" drug but is also used in robberies.

There was one nightclub in Riga, Latvia where it was common knowledge that visitors who flashed their money and Rolex's around could end up drugged and robbed, they would wake up in the morning somewhere missing their valuables. When they reported the robberies to the police they would not take the victims seriously, what was to prove they did not drink themselves unconscious, the victim could not remember what they were doing, so they could have given their valuables away etc. As long as no-one got hurt the police in Riga weren't concerned. Currently while writing this chapter the police in West Palm Beach and Broward Counties in South Florida are looking for a gang of females who have been drugging men in bars and nightclubs and robbing them.

You don't have the go to nightclubs to be exposed to the risk of being drugged, one Gypsy tactic in Europe is to get their small children to go out and sell glasses of tea or soft drinks to tourist, who would expect a little girl to give you a spiked drink. The children are accompanied by teenagers who then watch and follow the victim until they passed out or go and help them when they start to stumble at which time they rob them.

Rohypnol/Flunitrazepam is a tasteless and odorless drug; Flunitrazepam takes approximately 15 to 20 minutes to take effect and usually lasts four to six hours, depending on dosage. The drug makes individuals unable to remember what happened while under the influence of the drug. Flunitrazepam is commonly used in sexual assaults; victims may not be able to recall the assault, the assailant and be uncertain about the facts surrounding the assault.

Even street criminals can plan and organize their crimes to a very high standard. This is best illustrated by something I witnessed in Central London in the mid-1990s. After working for a while on a surveillance job you get to know who is who in an area. Central London, like most, cities has a constant stream of people coming and going but it does not take time to identify the locals. We identified a group of teenage boys who were obviously living off streets. Their favorite hangout was around a Dunkin Doughnut shop and there was usually at least three of the group in the vicinity. It was not unusual for members of the group to leave the area with older men and then be followed by other members of their group in what could be classed as a classic formal foot surveillance formation. I was clear to us they were "Rent Boys", or male prostitutes. Later, when we mentioned this to the local police and they knew how these kids were operating but could do little to stop them.

How these kids operated was that when one had picked up a client they took them to a quiet local parking garage, the other members of their crew would follow. When the client and the "Rent Boy" were engaged in a sexual act, the others would appear, rough up the client and take his wallet and whatever other valuables he had on him.

The local police regularly got men, usually tourists or from outside of London, putting in reports that they were mugged in the car park where these kids took their clients. Before the police took things further they informed the men that they know this area was frequented by male prostitutes and then asked if they wanted to continue with this report- they usually did not.

These street kids knew there was a very high chance that the victim would not take things further with the police and press charges as they would have to explain why they were in a car park which was frequented by male prostitutes. The street kids' defense would be to let it be known that the victim had in fact solicited them for sex, which is illegal. So, if the victim pressed charges, it would be very likely that he would ruin his reputation, career, marriage and then be open to having charges pressed against him for solicitation, sex with a minor and public indecency. As you see from this story when apparently law-abiding people, who think they know what they are doing, cross the line into the criminal world, they are asking for trouble and many rightfully get it.

These street kids were at the lowest level of the criminal world. They managed to repeatedly and successfully rob outwardly respectable, professional men and then avoid prosecution from the law because they planned their operation properly. So, how do you think the professionals will do things when there a thousands of dollars at stake?

It is a fact of life that people have vices and I do not judge people on what they do in private, as long as it is between consenting adults. I have been asked quite a few times why I discuss prostitution etc. on my courses. I discuss these issues as they are areas where unwary people can and do get themselves into a lot of trouble. A consideration when hiring bodyguards is whether they are mature and streetwise, many are not.

I was once talking to someone who I know was working in the celebrity security business in Miami and they told me in detail about the one time they had gotten drunk in their life, this concerned me. At this time, I was used to dealing with the emerging markets of the 90's Eastern Europe where everyone drank alcohol and business meetings took place or usually ended up in strip bars and nightclubs. My concern with using this guy was what if he had to work with a client in an environment where drinking a little alcohol and going to clubs is expected. Would he be focused, alert and protecting his client, or getting drunk, falling in love with a stripper or just joining the party, I have seen this happen. Criminals will target your bodyguards first, remove the bodyguards, one way or another and you can then do what you want to their client.

In most places prostitution is illegal but, in some places, it is a licensed business. Even where it's illegal, you will not have to look far to find sex for sale, I am sure there are sex ad's online and escort agencies in the yellow pages for the area that you're in now. In some places you will get girls phoning your hotel room offering their services; your details having been supplied by their associates working in the hotel or the concierge can arrange girls for you, everyone is making a percentage of any deals that the prostitutes makes.

The main problems that come with prostitution are of course disease but also robbery and blackmail. If the prostitutes can get your hotel room details, I am confident that for a few dollars more those that manage them can get your hotel registration details, which will more than likely include your home address, business address and credit card details. How much would most businessman pay to stop the photos or video from their hotels security cameras showing him and a young lady getting cozy in the hotel bar and then going to his room being sent to his wife? Get the picture?

Another criminal tactic which involves sex is the "honey trap". This is where, let's say a female (The Bait) will approach and start a conversation with a male (Target), who may be a pre-planned target or just a businessman who looks like he has money. The aim of the female is to get the male to go with them to a hotel room or apartment for sex. If the male goes with her then the trap can develop in several ways. A crude honey trap would be where the target is drugged or beaten and then robbed. A more intricate honey trap would involve the target being videoed having sex with the bait, the more deviant the better and then blackmailed for business favors or hard currency. Some honey traps can go on for an extended period and can form into what the target believes is a relationship; this will continue until the controllers behind the bait get the information or results they are after. Another criminal tactic is to use a mature looking but underage girl or boy as bait, that way they have a lot of leverage on the target how has without knowing committed a serious criminal act, sex with a minor.

I have used the example of a female approaching a male, but it can work all ways, male to female, male to male, female to female etc. During the Cold War the East German "Stasi" successfully used male gigolos to target female secretaries working in influential posts in the West German government. It's believed the Stasi sex-spies managed penetrated all levels of the West German government, intelligence agencies and NATO command.

A contemporary and imaginative honey trap happened to a French businessman in 2002. This gentleman had met and had been exchanging messages with an attractive Russian female over the internet and agreed to go to Moscow to meet her in real life and spend some time with her. She met him at Sheremetyevo airport and took him to a waiting car where he was kidnapped- she had been working with a criminal gang! The first thing the Frenchman's wife knew about him going to Moscow was when she received a ransom demand for three million dollars. Luckily, the criminals were not that professional or brutal and Frenchman was rescued by the Moscow police. This case made the international media, now think about the damage it done to this Frenchman's personal and business credibility, not to mention how he would explain the situation to his wife.

A more common and accepted side of the sex industry are the strip bars. They can be found in most places some are respectable and well-run businesses, but others are not. If you must go to a strip bar do your research and go to one of the higher profile ones. One type of scam which is often used in smaller strip bars or clip joints is to vastly overcharge on drinks. For example, a man may go into one of these places and order a drink, say a Coke, and then possibly buy a drink for one of the hostesses. When he is presented with the bill, however, he finds it to be for a few hundred dollars. When he protests he is confronted by a couple of thugs who shows him the price list for drinks, which is well-hidden behind the bar. It is not unusual for a glass of Coke to be 3 to 4 hundred dollars. How things develop will depend on the club and the victim. In most cases the victim will have his wallet emptied and may be escorted to an ATM machine and instructed to draw out more money or just beaten and robbed. If there is more than one victim, one may be held in the venue while the other is sent to get more money. These operations rely on the fact that the people going into these places will not report these incidents to the police as they would not want people, such as their wives and bosses to know that they were in a sleazy strip bar in the first place.

In most countries, recreational drugs, such as heroin and cocaine, are illegal. Drugs mean problems- full stop! Being caught with illegal substances will land you in a lot of trouble and the fact that you are a foreigner could make things even worse for you. I am sure in most places the local authorities would love to make an example of you. To buy the drugs, you must first associate with street criminals, which opens you up to the threats of robbery and blackmail. Why should the dealer only take $40 off you for a bag of drugs, when he can take everything you have on you and still keep the drugs? If this happens, what are you going to do? Tell the police the guy you were buying drugs off robbed you? The only people who benefit from drugs deals are the dealers. I have never understood why people take drugs, some people are fussy about what they eat but will put unidentified chemicals in their body they bought from a scummy street criminal.

In most countries, alcohol is legal and is regularly available. Alcohol is the oldest and most extensively used drug in the world and the amount of alcohol-related problems are vast. If you must drink know your limitations and never overdo it, especially in an unfamiliar environment. Street criminals look for easy targets; people who have drunk too much are easy targets. Even though drunks may believe that they can take on the world, they can't. Alcohol makes you unsteady on your feet and slows your reactions; these are two of the main things you need to defend yourself. The street term, "Rolling Drunks", comes from the fact that to rob a drunk you just have to give them a push and roll them over to take their wallet.

Alcohol also lowers people's inhibitions and can cause the usually responsible businessman to accept the offer of company from a young lady calling their hotel room after they return from celebrating a successful business meeting, then the fun can commence but it may be short lived for the businessman!

Kidnappings & Assassinations

I have linked kidnapping and assassination together, because the initial planning for both crimes is the same. We will talk more about kidnappings in a later chapter; here you will learn how criminals would plan such crimes.

If you are working in any of the emerging markets of Africa, Latin America or Eastern Europe, you need to be aware of the threat of kidnapping. The fact that you are a foreigner is enough to make you a target, as does the fact you are wearing expensive clothing and jewelry. In some places, if the criminals can make a few hundred dollars off you, they will be happy. The days are gone when only wealthy and high-profile people were targeted for kidnapping.

Most people should never be faced with the threat of being targeted for assassination. In some of the emerging markets assassination is the unofficial way of solving business disputes, assassins are cheaper to hire than lawyers! I tell my clients that I place the threat from blackmail and kidnapping a lot higher than that of assassination. Think about it, if someone is executed what use are they, none! They have just been removed from the equation. If someone can be entrapped, blackmailed and manipulated they can provide the criminals with an ongoing source of funds or information etc. If someone is kidnapped, they are an asset which can be sold for a ransom. You must take all this into consideration when faced with business problems in the emerging markets, even if the disputes are over a minor amount of funds or assets.

Now we will talk about the main points of how a criminal group plans a kidnapping or assassination. If a criminal group is looking for sporadic targets of opportunity for an express kidnapping, they would have been looking for nearly the same characteristics in their victim as a mugger. The criminals will watch you to see if you look like you are worth kidnapping, listen to which languages you speak to shop keepers or waiters, what is your level of personal security, and can you defend yourself? The easiest way to assess someone's personal security is to go up to them and ask them a question, like what's the time. The criminals will be able to assess from your reaction and body language if you are security aware or not. Always be suspicious of strangers, male or female, who approach and talk to you, even if they seem nice. You must always be aware of your surroundings and watch for anyone following or watching you, if you see the same person several times in different locations start to take precautions and be ready for a problem.

If a criminal group is specifically targeting you for a kidnapping or assassination, they will need to select a time, place and method to carry out their plans. To do so, they will need to build a picture of your routine and lifestyle. They will be looking for a pattern in your daily schedule, so that they can predict when you will be at a certain place, at a certain time so, they can then kidnap or assassinate you.

It is difficult for people not to form predictable routines; humans are creatures of habit. The most common places for kidnappings or assassinations to take place are at the victim's place of business, their residence or when they are in or around their vehicles. Almost every day you will be at least one of these locations- if not all three. The criminals will want to assess your standard of personal security; for instance, are you armed, do you use security personnel and are they competent, does your home have alarms or watch dogs?

The primary way to get this type of information on someone is to put them under surveillance. Methods of surveillance vary and can include getting people to watch and follow the targets or using remote listening devices and cameras in their place of business, home or vehicle. With today's technology, surveillance techniques can also include hacking a target's computer and intercepting their e-mails. Think about it: if you were going to a foreign country on business and a criminal intercepted your e-mails for a week or so before you left, they would probably have a very good idea of your whole itinerary.

These days most people have at least one computer and when traveling take a laptop. Think about how many people can access your computer, for example colleagues at the office. If you leave you leave your computer at the office overnight can maintenance, security or cleaning staff get access to it. There have been cases of corporate espionage where private detective companies have placed agents in the cleaning and security staff working at their targets offices, so they can access the target company's computers and trash after work hours. Most people would not consider the threat from fat and bumbling night shift security guard downloading business data from their PC and copying papers, but you should! When you're traveling do you leave your laptop in your hotel room and is it password protected? You cannot carry your computers around with you all the time so, one thing to do is to keep minimum information on it, keep all your sensitive information on a thumb drive, which you can always keep on your person. Then if someone accesses your computer or it's lost or stolen the criminals won't get any worthwhile information.

Another common way to gain information on someone, a technique which is used by criminal, intelligence and law enforcement agencies alike, is to go through their targets garbage. These days a lot of people shred sensitive papers to prevent identity theft, but do they shred their grocery store recites, which have time, date and location on them? For example, if over a three-week period, the criminals were able to find receipts from a local grocery store in your garbage, which show a checkout time between 10 am and 11 am for the past three Saturday mornings, they would have identified a potential routine. On the next Saturday, it would make sense for the criminals to send someone to the grocery store at nine o'clock in the morning to wait and see if you turned up, who were you with, and where you parked your car and if you are paying attention to the environment. They could also use this opportunity to test your security by getting a young lady to ask you for help carrying her bags to her car.

All sensitive paperwork needs to be destroyed; shredded papers can be put back together, so you need to ensure they are burned. Another method is to soak the papers in water until the ink runs and the paper turns to mush.

Criminals will also look to recruit or blackmail your employees to give them your itinerary and information on your business- that's why you must insure that all you employees are vetted out, supervised by trusted personnel and all sensitive information is kept on a need to know basis. I do not blame people that are forced by criminals to provide information on their employers, in the emerging markets a lot of times they have little choice but to comply with the criminal's demands. The initial approach usually offers the employee cash or favors if they assist the criminals, if they reject the offers then family members will be contacted directly and threatened with violence or sexual assault. What's the employee to do, go to the police, who in many places fear, or working with the criminals. Consider what you would do if you are working in a volatile Latin American country and you find out that one of your employee's daughters has been threatened with being gang raped if the employee does not give the criminals your travel schedule. This is not a joke, consider what you would do!

If the threat is coming from, say, a known business rival, or if you frequently meet personally with new clients the criminal will just have to arrange a meeting with you at a place suitable for the kidnapping or assassination. Meetings should be considered high risk as people know where you will be at a specific time; we will discuss this more in a later chapter. When the criminals have identified your routine and have chosen a place to kidnap or assassinate you, they will then have to choose a method. If your threat is from professional criminals, and you do not identify that you are being targeted before the criminal's strike, the chances are you will be successfully kidnapped or assassinated. You must learn to identify and avoid potential problems, forget martial arts and Hollywood fight scenes; if it gets to the stage where you having to fight the chances are you have screwed up somewhere or are somewhere you shouldn't be. There are usually two outcomes of fights, someone goes to prison and someone goes to hospital, in the 3rd world you defiantly don't want to go to prison but if you don't, there is a very good chance you'll be going to the morgue.

For one article I wrote for a professional magazine in interviewed Stephen Langley who served with the British Royal Military police for over 14 years and has worked as corporate investigator, a senior security and crisis manager for a large international corporation, he is now the owner of Unique Global Consultancy Ltd. I asked Stephen what the problems were some of his clients have encountered while traveling and what advice would he give to travelers these days.

Firstly, I tell my clients to try to blend in with their environments, don't stand out and look like someone who is worth robbing. This might sound simply but can be a problem when we have European clients who do business in say East Africa, they can't change their skin color so, they are going to stand out. In these situations, we ensure their trips are planned in detail from who is picking them up at the airport, ensuring their hotels are secure and having a crisis plan in place. But always remember, we can make all the plans in the world, but we still must consider the human factor that a lot of people won't follow the plan for whatever reason. I remember one client arrived at Jomo Kenyatta International Airport in Nairobi and his arranged driver was late, so he took a taxi to his hotel. Well the taxi driver pulled off the main road after leaving the airport, stopped and aggressively demanded $100 dollars from the client as the fare to take him to his hotel, this was well over what the fare should have been, but the client was terrified and handed over £100 pounds, he never had dollars... The client was luckily dropped off at his hotel unharmed, it was not worth informing the police as there was no evidence of anything more than a dispute about the taxi fare. I stress to female clients to always use the drivers or car services we arranged or approved for them as they run the risk of sexual assault and not just robbery.

Another area where people have problems is where they socialize after work hours and this can be a big problem in US, Europe or Africa. You can tell your clients to dress down and not wear expensive watches etc. but they always will, and such things can draw the attention of criminals. Internationally there has been a big increase in drugs being used in robberies, the criminals will identify their target in a bar or night club, if the target is male they will send a young lady to talk with them and when they are distracted spike their drinks with some form of drug that will knock them out. Its common knowledge that date rape drugs are used by men who want to sexually assault women, but they are also increasingly being used against men for sexual assault and robbery. The drugs used incapacitate the victim who cannot protect themselves, remember the details of being robbed or raped. In many places the police will dismiss the cases as there is little evidence and even if caught the criminal can claim the victim gave them their valuables or the sex was consensual. For the victims they are lucky if they have just lost their valuables and money, if they have been sexually assaulted they have to deal with the trauma of the attack, possible sexually transmitted diseases and pregnancies...

Being drugged is not only confined to night clubs, I was approached by one client who sought training after he had an incident while visiting the Grand Bazaar in Istanbul. He had bought tea from a vendor and shortly afterwards began to feel light headed, he noticed he was being watched by several young men and made his way to the street and flagged down a taxi. At this point one of the young men tried to pull him away from the taxi but, even though this gentleman was in his late 50's he was 6 feet, 2 inches tall, 270 pounds, a former rugby player and able to push the young man away the get into the taxi. The taxi took him to his hotel where a doctor was called, and it was found out he had been poisoned with ketamine. He was lucky because the doctor believed the dosage used on him was not enough to take full effect but would have been enough to knock out a smaller man or woman. When I asked the client about the incident it became clear why he had been targeted, he was carrying an expensive Nikon camera and wearing a Bvlgari watch and sunglasses, overall a little over ten thousand dollars' worth valuables to start with...

So, for me the emphasis for all security operations is a thorough threat assessment, a realistic security plan and briefing the clients on the potential threats they can encounter. I can only do so much, when the clients are traveling I am not going to be with them most of the time and they must be able to look after themselves. I always have a crisis response plan ready for my clients, but my aim is to properly manage their travels and prepare them, so we never need to use it!

Advance Security

Advance security is a necessity in all security operations. It can take two forms and may be performed covertly or overtly. It is essential in the planning and operational phases and should be employed whenever the time and manpower are available.

Advance security in the planning phase

When planning an operation, it pays to have someone go to all the locations that you will be visiting in advance. Once there, they will need to make a threat assessment of all the potential threats that might occur and how to avoid them and, if necessary, counter them. If you are going to a foreign country, your advance person or team should make sure that the hotels are suitable, select routes between venues, make first aid arrangements, confirm your communications work, and arrange transportation. These days' videos and photos can be e-mailed back by the advance person or team so the main body of travelers and get a feel for location before they arrive.

Advance security in the operational phase

Advance security in the operational phase of an operation is extremely important and should be employed if you have the necessary manpower, if you are traveling on your own you could possibly hire a local but, will you be able to trust them. If you are traveling in a group you should take turns at being the advance person, if there is a problem it's better to lose only one person rather than the whole group.

The job of the advanced person or team in the operational phase is to proceed you by 10 to 20 minutes and check the route and final location for potential threats and problems. If any threats or problems are detected, the advance person or team will inform you immediately, so that you can go to the secondary plan. For example: We were once working with a client who was going to a potentially hostile South American country, he initially wanted us to supply him with firearms for when he was traveling around the country. But when we made clear the problems that can come with carrying firearms / weapons in a foreign country he began to see the difference between the real world and Hollywood. We organized an advance man for him to arrange his hotel, pick him up from the airport and who would precede him on his travels in a vehicle that fitted in with those being used by the locals. Our operative would inform the client of any problems or anything suspicious along the routes. When he arrived at a location ahead of the client he would check for any threat surveillance personnel etc. Of course, our operative was Latin American in appearance, fluent in Spanish and trained by us.

It is best that all advance work is performed covertly. If a venue or location needs to be checked out, the advance person or team can always claim that they are representing someone else or that they want to hire the venue or stay in the hotel themselves. By performing this duty covertly, they will not give away your itinerary. When performing advance security, wear what helps you to blend in with the environment. There is a fixation in the security and business world that personnel must wear a suit, shirt and tie, this is OK in New York or London but in many countries, you will just stand out from the crowd and make yourself a target. If you look like a business person everyone will think you have money and worth taking the time to rob or kidnap. Always try to dress down and blend in with the people around you.

Personal Security in Hotels

It is inevitable that in the close protection business you will spend time in domestic and international hotels of some description. Always do your research online before booking a hotel; research crime statistics, ratings from others who have stayed there and check out the area with Google Earth. If your hotel has been booked for you by your company still research the place and if you find potential issues get them to change it.

Over the years I have stay and worked in a wide variety or hotels from five-star to minus-star and boutique to roach house. The standard or security in most hotels is very low and it is not hard for non-hotel residents to go up onto the hotel floors. It's concerning that most travelers expect and believe the hotels they are staying in to be secure, I tell my clients they should take the same precautions inside hotels as they would on the street.

A lot of hotels do not have security personnel, a lot of times they give the security job title to the concierge staff so, on paper they have security personnel and can keep the insurance costs down for the hotel. Even in large five-star hotels they usually only have one security person on duty at a time. In my experience, the standard of hotel security personnel can range from good to appalling. There is one large high-profile London hotel where the only reason they have a security team is to keep their insurance costs down. The hotel has 14 miles of corridor, over 1000 rooms, multiple entrances and there is only one unmotivated security person on at a time- in a place like this you are on your own. Security is usually low on a hotels managements list of priorities, as they are more interested in keeping their rooms full. Most hotels will only do the minimum to comply with local security regulations and keep their insurers happy.

One story that highlights the failings of hotel security happened in the late 90's at a five-star hotel on the exclusive Sloane Street in central London. The hotel policy was that when the female maids were cleaning the guest's rooms they had to leave the room doors open for their own personal security, they were not supposed to be in a room alone with a guest.

An experience hotel thief was in the hotel and walking the floors; he was dress in a decent suit with a brief case and looked very corporate. He entered a room which was being cleaned and ask the maid to finish up as he wanted to take a shower, the maid thinking the thief was the guest who was staying in the room finished and left. In a lot of five-star hotels staff won't challenge guests as it is not polite to do so, it's all about service.

Now the thief was in the room and took anything of value, this guy was a professional and he did not finish there. He telephoned the hotel reception from the room phone and told them he had forgotten the combination to the safe in the room, guest forgetting combinations and safe's malfunctioning is something that happens quite often. So, reception got the duty security guard to go up and open the safe for the thief; the security guard believed the thief was a guest as he was in the room semi-dressed and watching TV. The guard opened the safe told the thief how to reprogram the combination and politely left room. The thief then emptied the safe and left the hotel. This happened during the day, professional hotel thieves usually operate during the day when hotel guests are out sightseeing or doing business. When the Japanese guests who were staying in the room returned in the evening they found all their valuables were gone and were not very happy, especially when they found out that the hotel security staff had assisted the thief in the robbery.

It used to amuse me when I was working in the five-star hotels in central London how everything on the surface seemed to be of the highest standard but if you looked behind the scenes it was another story. Several of the top hotels were using a temp agency that was renowned for using illegal immigrants to supply them with back of house staff such as dish washers etc. This temp-agency was cheap and it's all about saving pennies, right? There would Royalty and Politicians upstairs eating Beluga caviar and undocumented workers downstairs opening the tins.

I was once talking with a hotel security manager in London who had just taken over the security for a very prominent five-star hotel. He was stressed because he had gone through computer that was used for programming staff key cards and found there were over 50 master keys for hotel issued, that were valid and a lot unaccounted for. There should only have been about four master key cards on issue for the general manager, duty manager, security manager and duty security. The reason there were so many master keys on issue was because it was easier to program a card for all areas rather than the specific floors and rooms the individual staff members needed. Most hotels use electronic key cards but how many reprogram locks and void lost key cards, or those guests have not handed in when they checked out. So, combine the fact that anyone can walk into most hotels and they might have a valid key card they have found or bought from an employee how secure do you think you are in most hotels, same as if you're on the street.

Another example of hotel crime took place several years ago to my business partner in Caracas who was providing security for a lady who was visiting for several weeks; he picked her up from the airport and was escorting her around the city. She was staying in a very good hotel and when he was not with her she was in her hotel suite. After a week or so this lady started to get threatening text messages on her cell phone from someone asking for a large sum of money. This was baffling to us as the lady had been keeping a very low profile so, an operation was initiated, and the potential extortionist entrapped. It turned out the extortionist worked in the hotel, he was the Fed-ex man and got the ladies cell phone number and details from a package she had received. This wannabe criminal was fired from his job and the police would have been happy to arrest him, but the lady thought him losing his job was enough punishment and did not press charges, he was very lucky.

So, hopefully you are beginning to see that security is not high on most hotels priority list. A lot of shady business takes place in hotels and they are choice locations for prostitutes, thieves and fraudsters. When selecting a hotel find one that provides you with comfort and security, I don't need five-star services so, tend to choose the smaller and quieter places where it is easy for strangers and non-residents to be spotted.

Security considerations for a hotel stay

- Complete a threat assessment on the hotel before your stay.
- Check to ensure the hotel is not in or close to any high crime areas
- Make sure the hotel is not near any other building that could have a threat against them such as police or military barracks, etc.
- Have a security plan and make sure everyone traveling with you knows it.
- Liaise with hotel staff and find out what security procedures they have in place, if they have cameras where are they located, do they work and are they recording.
- Try to check out other guests, you don't want to be staying near a high-risk VIP's, as if they are targeted you might get caught up in the incident.
- Your rooms should be above the second floor and at the end of a corridor; high enough so nothing can be thrown through the window but still within easy reach of fire fighters' ladders. And at the end of a corridor so you are

close to fire escapes and will not have to many people walking past your room.

- Locate possible criminal surveillance positions around the exterior of the hotel and monitor them.
- Keep an eye out for suspicious people in the public areas of the hotel.
- Search all rooms before occupation for electronic surveillance devices or contraband that could have been left by the previous guest.
- If possible let no one into your rooms unattended, use the do not disturb sign to keep out the maids.
- Do not let anyone in your room without confirming who they are with the hotel reception. Think about it, if a man turned up at your door in a security uniform, with an ID badge claiming to be hotel security and needed to talk to you would you open the door, most people would. Anyone can buy a uniform and you can make ID cards on your computer, always confirm someone's ID with the hotel reception.
- Work out how you can secure the hotel room, check to make sure the windows are lockable, if there is a balcony could someone climb or drop onto it. See if there is anything you can use to block the door such as a chair or table, if it won't stop an intruder it should at least be able to wake you up.
- There are numerous small and affordable security alarms on the market that can be used for a hotel room ranging from door and window alarms to motion detectors.
- If there is an incident are you going to fight or flee, is there a suitable safe room such as a bathroom and how long will you need to hold out until help arrives?
- Make plans for evacuating the hotel in the event of an emergency, remember do not use obvious evacuation routes as they could be booby trapped or ambushed.
- Check that your mobile/cell phone works and you are not in a signal dead spot.
- Will you have internet access, and will it be secure.
- Do not leave valuables in your hotel room; put them in the main hotel safe, if possible. Criminals can get master keys for hotel room safes.
- Do not throw sensitive information in the trash cans, soak and throw it away outside of the hotel or flush it down the toilet
- If your room has a fridge, do not use any ice cubes, as they could be spiked or poisoned as can any snacks and drinks.
- Always know where the nearest hospital is, what first aid equipment and first aid trained staff does the hotel have.

Attending Events

The reason for a lot of travel is to attend business events and social functions, these can prove to be troublesome, if not planned properly. Most function venues will have their own security personnel and procedures, the standard of these can range from quite good to accidents simply waiting to happen. I know of one very high-profile hotel in London that had all their banqueting furniture stolen by a group of men claiming they were there to pick the furniture up for cleaning, they loaded it all up into a truck in broad daylight and were never seen again.

Over the years I have provided security for a wide range of corporate events, meetings, social functions and encountered problems ranging from flooding, permitting issues, paparazzi, assaults, drug use and prostitution. As with hotels, most event organizers do not put a high priority on security and usually, at most may hire a guard or two to stand at the main entrance. I have worked VIP functions where Politicians and Royalty have been present by myself because the event organizers did not book more security personnel, at these events there was no way for one person to secure the venue. Luckily, nothing went wrong but I never understand why people will spend tens of thousands of dollars on organizing a function and consider security as an unnecessary expense. I am sure many of those attending such events expect a decent standard of security and would be concerned if they knew the real story.

One weak spot I have repeatedly seen, internationally, is that temporary staff are rarely profiled, vetted and in many cases are undocumented workers. A lot of large venues use temp agencies to supply them with dish washers, waiters and bar staff for functions; they do not keep such people on staff as they do not need them all the time. You can have metal detectors at the main entrance of a venue, every guest searched, every door in the venue manned by a trained and competent security person, but the chances are none of the regular and temp venue staff will be at searched and they are the ones that will be serving food, drinks, manning bag and coat checks.

As with everything else, do your threat assessment and do not trust others to have your security at the top of their priority list. Here is a list of things that you need to take into consideration when attending events.=

Considerations for attending an event

- Compile a threat assessment on the venue and consider who attending may have an active threat on them.
- Get the full postal address, contact numbers and a map grid number for the venue. Look on Google earth and assess the venue and the surrounding area.
- Consider if there are any building's around or on routes approaching the venue that could be targets for criminals or terrorists.
- Do you have the name and number of a contact person at the venue or with the event organizers who can answer any questions you might have?
- If possible send an advance person to check out the venue and the surrounding area, remind them to take plenty of photos and video of the layout of the place
- Examine, in detail, the layout of the building and note all: entrance and exit points, stairwells, elevators, escape routes and potential safe rooms.
- Will the venue have been searched for explosive devices and weapons, if yes, by whom and what security procedures have been put in since the search?
- What time will you arrive and is there a cut off time for entrance?
- How will you get to the venue, if you are driving where will you park and is the area secure?
- If invitations or tickets are required will they need to be shown on entry; who will responsible for looking after the invitations and tickets?
- If reservations or tickets need to be booked try not to use your name, use a company or cover name.
- What entrances will you use, what security is there, will you be searched and are those conducting the searches competent?
- Will you or anyone else be able to take weapons into the venue?
- What alternative entrances and exits are there, such as fire exits or those marked for staff?
- Give all entrances and exits code numbers so that if you need to evacuate you can communicate with your group or driver without anyone else knowing which exit and route you're using?
- If using a driver where will they be parked and how long will it take them to get to each exit, make sure they know the codes numbers for the exits.
- What facilities are there for drivers; food, drink and toilets etc.

- What facilities are there at or close to the venue; pay phones, bathrooms, restaurants, hotels, stores etc.
- What is the overall program for the event and what is your program.
- Where will you be seated, is a good position that has a good view of the venue and is close to exits?
- Do any other guests have threats on them, if yes, where will they be seated?
- Will you be dining and who will prepare the food?
- Do you or anyone one in your group have any special dietary requirements?
- If you are using bodyguards where will they be located and what, if any, are the dinning arrangements for them?
- Will media or photographers be present and what restrictions will be placed on them?
- Will security or police personnel be present, and will they be armed?
- Will security and police personnel be in uniform or plain clothes, if plain clothes will they be wearing any form of identification?
- Will guests and staff wear identification badges? Try to see or get examples of all types of identification so you can hopefully verify a fake from a real one.
- Will your communications work in the venue, what alternatives are there?
- What first aid facilities are available, where is the nearest hospital with an emergency room and what are the best routes to get there?
- What firefighting equipment is there at the venue, where is it located and is it serviceable?
- What are the response times for the emergency services for incidents ranging from a guest having a heart attack to a terrorist attack?
- Make plans and procedures for how you're going to react to all the threats you have identified in your threat assessment be it food poisoning or a terrorist attack.
- Make sure you know how to raise the alarm in the case of an emergency or anti-social behavior such as drug use or drunkenness etc.
- Find out what the venue's official evacuation procedures are and then make your own; in the case of a terrorist attack the terrorists would most probably know the official evacuation procedures and would have booby trapped or ambushed these exits and routes out of the venue.
- Plan escape routes to exits form all areas of the venue.
- Have code words within your group for emergencies as you do not want others to know what you're doing or where you're going.
- Is there a suitable location that could be used as a safe room and how long could you hold out there for?

- Allocate emergency rendezvous points outside of the venue and make sure everyone in you group knows them. These are important because if you group is separated during an evacuation you can quickly re-group again. Also, if you're using a driver and there is an emergency at the venue they may not be able to get close to pick you up due to traffic or a police cordon. It may be easier for you to walk a couple of blocks away from the venue where it would be less congested.
- Plan primary and secondary routes to your residence and safe houses from the venue.

You can see from this list that going to business and social functions can take some thinking about. As I stated in a previous most people are unaware of what is going on around them and when there is an emergency are clueless on how to react. You don't want to be one of these people and it does not take much effort not to be!

Dealing with fake police

Criminals impersonating police officers is a big problem internationally. So, what should people do if they are approached by someone claiming to be a police officer? Most police have people respect so, when someone claims to be a police officer they are believed. The criminals know this and that is why they try to impersonate police officers to commit their crimes. In this chapter we will look at the problem of police impersonators and give you some procedures to follow if you suspect a supposed police officer is not a real cop!

Firstly, we will look at the problem of criminal impersonating police in one of the most dangerous countries in the world, Mexico. I spoke with "Antonio" a former member of an elite Mexican police tactical team, GET of Leon, Guanajuato. We asked Antonio how big the problem of police impersonators was in Mexico and his response was, *"The problem is huge, it's extremely difficult to know who a real cop is and who are members of drug cartels. When on duty we could always check what patrols are in the area by radio, civilians cannot do this. Many of the drug cartels have corrupted police officers and have access to radios, uniforms and weapons, to be honest, a lot of the time they are better armed and equipped than the police. Especially in undercover operations we were always extremely careful when approaching a checkpoint manned by cops we did not know. When we got close we could easily identify the fake cops due to how they wore their uniforms, equipment, body language and their procedures. On high-risk prisoner escorts we always have a covert car ahead of us scouting the roads to ensure we did not drive into an ambush."*

Antonio detailed one kidnapping that was committed by police officers that were from another state in Mexico but were working a case in Guanajuato. Antonio said, "These two detectives were in Leon following up on a case from *Tamaulipas. They kidnapped a 16-year-old kid form a middle-class family, the kidnap was easy as they showed the kid their badges and faked an arrest, the kid was terrified and complied as he thought he was in trouble. The first we knew of the kidnapping was when the family came to the police with a video of the victim naked, bruised and being beaten. Luckily for the kid and the family we were able to identify the kidnappers as the police officers. We were able to do this because one of our people recognized the shoes in the video as being the same as what one of the cops was wearing. These cops turned kidnappers were put under surveillance, we got a positive ID on the shoes, we did a close reconnaissance on the villa where they were staying, and it was clear something was not right about the place. We raided the place and we found the kid alive but badly beaten, the two cops were arrested."* When asked what the outcome would have been for the kid if he was not rescued Antonio said, *"He would have been killed, even if the ransom would have been paid, those cops would not have risked releasing him as he could identify them"* When asked what the kid could have done when confronted by the cops, Antonio said, *"You know if you have committed a crime or not, if you know you're innocent then complain and call the police station. If nothing else let others know you are being arrested and ask them to report what's happening. If you have a cell phone use it, alert as many people as possible, this is not a game, it's life"*

The United Kingdom is a relatively safe country, and crime is nowhere near the scale it is in Mexico, but they still have a problem with police impersonators. The British Police are the oldest and most established in the world so, next I spoke with Peter Wheeler who has recently retired as a lead investigator from The British Police Force having completed 30 years' service. Peter is now a security consultant and instructor and provided us with a check list of considerations that can help identify if you're being stopped or contacted by a real police officer or not.

If pulled over while driving.

- Generally, police vehicles are easy to identify, if an undercover car is used then it should have blue flashing lights inside the grill area or magnetic types on roofs. Be more suspicious if stopped by an undercover car as these are easier to mimic.
- If you are pulled over, consider moving to or keeping in a busy well-lit area where members of the public are in view and can see what's going on.
- Real Police officers completing stops and checks will be in police uniform or will be wearing clearly identifiable police labelled clothing.
- Officers will be in possession of their identity card which contains a photograph of the officer. It's your right to ask to be shown their ID cards clearly and to check them.
- During initial contact keep all doors locked and lower your window a small amount to communicate through, always remain calm and be polite. This will also allow documents to be exchanged if required.
- If you decide not to stop, contact the Police as a matter of urgency to outline your concerns and seek guidance on how to proceed.

If you receive a phone call from someone claiming to be the police.

- Ask for the officer's identification number and the phone number of the Police Station you can call them back on. Check the Police Station telephone number against online listings before calling back and do not accept mobile numbers for verification call backs.
- Consider checking the incoming call number and recording it, make notes of the callers voice any background noise and content.
- If told to put the landline receiver down and call straight back do so on a separate line, it is not unknown for callers to keep the line open on their end thus tricking you into thinking you have completed a security check.
- Make an appointment to visit the officer at the Police Station to discuss the matter they called you about in person.
- If a home visit is requested, agree to an appointment and ask a friendly neighbor or family member to be present.
- Do not pass personal details about yourself, in particular Bank Account / PIN numbers, state you intend to contact the Bank directly to discuss matters.
- Refrain from being put under pressure to respond immediately, a few simple checks will not take long to complete, and a real police officer will understand your concerns.

If a police officer turns up at your residence

- A fake police officer wanting to gain access to your house may claim that you have been the victim of crime or likely to be in the near future, to put you under pressure to act quickly with little time to think.
- Always ensure all doors are locked and attempt to visually check the visitor prior to answering the door.
- Fit a door chain – and use it.
- If unsure do not answer the door.
- Call the Police and enquire the reason for the visit, if the visit is legitimate they will know and will tell you how to procced.
- Always ask for the officers' ID cards and check them, consider cross referencing some of the details on the card with the officer.
- Consider telling the officer to come back at a future time so you can arrange for a friend / family member to be present. This will also give you time to verify with the police station that the police officer is real!
- Be suspicious of items asked to be removed, ensure the officer has paperwork authorizing such and ensure a receipt is provided, consider taking photographs of both the items and officers responsible.

- Officers will not request that they take items for 'Safe Keeping'.
- Remember it is your home, so don't be embarrassed, do not allow anyone in who you are suspicious of, always verify their ID's and check with the police station that the visit is legitimate.

The basic rule is check the police officers' ID, if they are real they will show you their ID card, verify the reason the officer is stopping you or visiting you with their station if you are still suspicious. Now these days nearly everyone has a smart phone and we were interested in seeing if there were any applications or programs that could help someone identify if they were being stopped by a fake or real cop.

Andrew Chatzkelowitz is a very experienced security consultant, instructor and project manager who has worked in hostile environments throughout Africa, he is now based in Johannesburg, South Africa. South Africa is a beautiful country but is sadly plagued with very high rates of violent crime and criminals impersonating police officers is common. Mr. Chatzkelowitz again clarified the basics of what someone should do if they suspect they are stopped by a fake cop. He said, "Most of the criminals here that impersonate police tend to operate on the more remote and quiet stretches of road, they will target females and those they see as potentially easy targets. If someone is being stopped while driving we tell them to go to a busy area, such as a gas station or a mall, especially if it is a lone female. They should keep their doors locked and not get out the car until the police officer has been positively identified. If anyone tries to break into the car they need to drive to the nearest police station or safe area as quickly and safely as they can. One situation where people are vulnerable is when their cars break down in remote or not the best areas, they need to summon help as soon as possible, keep their doors locked and not get out of the vehicle. People should have a plan in place for all potential hazard and problems they could encounter."

Mr. Chatzkelowitz went on to inform us that the South African Police had developed a free smartphone app called "Namola" (https://namola.com/) which alerts the emergency services that you have a potential problem or are being a victim of a crime. Mr. Chatzkelowitz said, "Namola gives you a direct line to the emergency services, when you hit the panic button they will call you back immediately to see what your problem is, assess your situation and give you advice. If it's the case of a fake cop they will be able to clarify this immediately and send real police units to your assistance. They know your location because the app works with the GPS on your phone, there are other features to the app but the panic button alone can be a life saver."

So, we have spoken with experts from 3 different countries and 3 very different environments and their basic response to what you should do if approached by a suspicious person claiming to be a police officer are the virtually the same: check their ID's and call the police verify their identifications and reason for stopping you. To summarize what we have discussed in the article, if you are stopped or approached by a police officer you need to ask yourself the following questions:

- What crime have you committed, if none then why are they stopping you?
- Does the officer's car look like a police car?
- Does the officer look like a police officer, does he have the right uniform or identification visible?
- What is his body language saying, is he nervous or calm and professional?
- Can he provide you with and let you check his ID card that will have his photo and personal details on it?
- Will he allow you to call the police station to verify his identity or allow a friend to be present while he questions you?

If the answers to the above questions are negative the chances are you are dealing with a fake cop. You need to remain calm and polite and try to summon help, if you have your phone dial a trusted friend or the police so at least they can hear what is going on if you cannot talk directly to them. Try to detail the situation, that you need help and your location, keep repeating this... If the situations becomes violent and it is clear the man is not a police officer and is attempting to kidnap you then resist, fight, shout and scream and do everything you can to alert people that you are being attacked!

As soon as you possibly can after being approached by someone suspicious or being attacked contact the police or a trusted person and let them know your location and what happened. If possible try to get photos or video of the criminal with your phone's camera, if you can't try to remember as much as you can about them. Take note of make and model of their car, if the car had any dents anything distinguishing. When trying to describe a person remember their height, if fat or skinny, their color and accent. Also, anything distinguishing such as scars, tattoos, jewelry, how they smell and their shoes... Very few people wear the same shoes, and this can be a good identification point.

Driving in Hostile Areas

January 2013 and I am sitting in the back of a Toyota Prada on the outskirts of ill-famed Cité Soleil in Port-au-Prince, Haiti, which is regarded as one of the poorest and most dangerous slums in the Western Hemisphere. My Haitian operatives are doing a deal with a local senior gang member; a chubby kid in his early 20's wearing an Ed Hardy T-shirt and big, white sunglasses, who was sitting outside of a dirt floored plywood shack, mingling with several other local young ladies and gentlemen... We needed to go into Cité Soleil to perform an advance reconnaissance on a location our VIP client would be visiting the next day; not a recommended area for a day trip but since they were paying the bills it was their choice. The deal was done and for a few dollars we had a local kid ride with us, acting as our guide and ticket of good faith.

During my long career I have been in such situations numerous times and the threat of being set-up, ambushed etc. is always present but that goes with the turf. I am sure it was clear to the teenage gangbanger who was sitting next to me that if things went bad he would be the first to be gut shot; if I was going to suffer, so was he! I am certain I was the only white guy for a few miles around and the odds of me making it out would have been slim... such is life, I chose to be there. Having served in Northern Ireland with the British Army in the late 80's and early 90's the murders of Corporals Howes and Wood(s) in Belfast, 1988 emphasized how vulnerable a vehicle is when trapped by a violent mob and how your reaction must be fast and aggressive. Corporals Howes and Woods wrongly drove into an Irish Republican Terrorist's funeral procession and were attacked by the mob, dragged from their vehicle, beaten, driven to waste ground, stripped and executed with their own weapons.

After about half an hour later it became clear that the location we were looking for was not in Cité Soleil. After numerous phone calls it was confirmed the site was a few miles outside the slum in greener pastures. This is a perfect illustration for the necessity of advance security procedures. This client set himself apart from many others by spending a few extra dollars and getting things done in advance, properly thus avoiding any potential issues.

Safe Driving

Over the 29-year span of my career I have seen little need for evasive driver training but have seen the need for people to learn how to handle vehicles at high speed and in hazardous weather conditions. The main thing you need to learn is how to drive safely, be able to identify any possible threats and how to avoid them. In most large towns and cities, you will not be able to perform such things as J turns or other evasive maneuvers due to lack of space and heavy traffic, so you must always be aware of what is going on around you. My primary advice to people is to keep as much space as possible between themselves and the car in front, as this can give you some space to maneuver in congested traffic. When you are driving look around and always be thinking of where you could take evasive action; in urban areas there will be few places where you could spin your car 180 degrees and drive against the traffic flow; that's Hollywood, not reality!

If the criminals or terrorists are in anyway professional, they will attack you when your car is penned in and you cannot perform any evasive maneuvers, not on wide open roads. It's common street kid tactics in a lot of Latin American cities to rob cars at traffic lights that are at least two cars back from the stop light with other cars behind them; these cars are stuck and cannot escape. If street kids on bicycles with rusty revolvers have worked out how to jack people in cars, don't you think their big brothers have also? One such story came out of Latin America; a top competition shooter was driving to work one day when two kids on a motorcycle pulled up next to him while he was stuck in traffic. The kid on the back of the bike had a revolver and asked the competition shooter at gun point for his wallet; he complied. As he was handing over the wallet he reached for the Walther PPK on his ankle. The kid saw the gun, shot and killed him. Who was the better shot that day, the trained or the street wise?

Another important thing to consider when working with vehicles is the type of ammo you carry in your pistols; if you have the choice full metal jacket rounds could be a better option versus hollow points as they penetrate better through windshields and doors etc. A good example of HP rounds not penetrating enough happened to a close friend and associate of mine in 2010 when he was robbed, and car jacked by two wanted armed criminals on the Caribbean island where he lives. He did a good job and managed to deploy his 9mm Sig-Pro that the criminals failed to find when they frisked him. The shooting started when the attackers tried to make their getaway in his truck. The result was that one of them died and the other survived even though critically wounded. The reason one survived was because he was shielded from the police recommended 124 grain hollow point rounds my associate was shooting by the frame of the car and the seats. The rounds went through the frame and hit him several times in the head, but without enough power to penetrate the skull and kill him. I believe that if my associate had mixed in a few full metal jacketed rounds in his magazines there would have been two dead criminals that day.

It always amazes me to still see police and security personnel using out of date Israeli style procedures and not keeping a round chambered in their weapons. Basics, always fully load your weapon and put a round in the chamber. Your reactions must be fast and aggressive!

While I was in Nigeria in 2012 there was one incident where three police officers were killed in what we believe to be an attempted assassination of the VIP they were escorting. While on a busy and congested road the policemen exited their truck and approached a car that was blocking it and their client's vehicle's route; as they got close one of the criminals opened up on them with an AK-47and all three died at the scene. The officers who were all carrying AK's with the safety catches on and no rounds in the chambers approached in a bunch, did not use cover and they did not stand a chance. The client's vehicle was hit and one of their children was wounded. Consequently, the criminals ran out of ammo and ran into the crowd. One of the vehicles that was involved in the incident was hit once in the engine and that was enough to stop it. These days there are so many computers in a vehicle's engine that if one is damaged the car will just stop running!

In a perfect world engines should be armored but the main issues would be the client's willingness to pay for this, the availability of materials and mechanics to do the job and a lot of times the answer will be "NO". I am regularly asked by my clients whether I favor armored cars or not. In my opinion, as it is with everything else, they have their pros and cons. Armored cars do have an application and the first thing you need to consider is what level of armoring the vehicle you're buying or using has. I have come across people driving around in cars armored to stop pistol caliber rounds in areas where the bad guys carry assault weapons. They thought an armored car was all they needed and were unaware of the different levels of armoring. You will also need to confirm where the car is protected; doors, windows, floor, engine, roof etc. Because some vehicles may only have some armored panels in the doors and rear seat, it is necessary to always check for yourself and not take anybody's word for it.

Now think like the criminals, if you knew your target was driving around in a SUV armored to B6 level are you going to shoot at them when they are in route or wait for them stop and get out of the vehicle or stop them and make them get out of their vehicle? Think about how can you get someone out of a car; what would you do if a female driver bumped into the back of your car? Would you get out to inspect the damage and thus possibly be kidnapped by her two-armed accomplices crouched in the back seat of her car? Always be aware of decoys that are intended to make you stop and get out of your vehicle, such as accidents or even bodies next to the road. Basic rule: stay in your car and keep moving between safe areas.

A criminal tactic in Europe when targeting armored cash-in-transit vehicles is to box them in, cover the van in gasoline, then give those inside the option of throwing out the cash, surrendering or being burnt alive. An issue with armored vehicles is that you cannot shoot at the criminals from the inside. There was one incident I recall from the mid 1990's where an unarmored van that was moving cash was stopped and ambushed in an Eastern European country. The fact that the van was unarmored enabled the security personnel inside to shoot through the side of the van and fight off the attackers, which they could not have done if they had taken and armored van that day. There have also been numerous incidents where criminals have assassinated targets traveling in armored vehicles using Improvised Explosive Devices (IEDs), Rocket Propelled Grenades (RPGs) and improvised shaped charges. An armored vehicle can assist you in your security program, but it should not be all there is to it. Basic advance security and route selection still have to be applied.

In January 2013 my business partner in Caracas, Venezuela was attacked while driving his armored Land Cruiser. This is a good example of how sporadic incidents can happen in seconds in places like Caracas and how a professional response can save lives. The criminals in this case were car jackers or express kidnappers who trawl the streets looking for victims. His vehicle was shot fourteen times and if they hit it fourteen times I am sure they missed another fourteen. This also serves as a good example to emphasize that the bad guys have no intention to play with you, they mean business!

Here is my partner's description of the incident: *We just left the client at the hotel and I was taking my partner R who was riding escort to his friend's house. A red Toyota Hilux with five guys stopped beside me at the red light. They pointed a Glock at my window. I accelerated, and they started following and shooting. I hit the brakes, so they could smash the car against my rear fender buy didn't work. They stopped as well. After a barrage of shots, they stopped, I supposed they were reloading. I was ten meters away in front of them when I said, "OK MY TURN NOW!" But they kept shooting and by now I didn't know how much the rear window was going to resist, so I had to move and could not shoot back, their fire was too heavy, and they did not follow. I just got that armored Land Cruiser from my cousin one month ago. I knew sooner or later this was going to happen. They shot the gas tank and I was losing fuel. I left R fast and I went back home the same direction to see if they were still there but nothing. I lost all the fuel and barely made it home. It pissed me off, boss. I could not even shoot one of them.*

Luckily no one was hurt in this incident. I expect the fact the vehicle was armored and that he hit the breaks for them to hit him let the attackers know they were not playing with an amateur. Criminals want easy targets, don't be one!

In my professional opinion for me there is a lot more you need to be aware of when providing protection services and working with vehicles than just being a good driver. In the narrow-congested city streets or the flooded, pot holed dirt roads of today's emerging markets you need to be thinking chess not checkers. Maybe because I am an infantryman at heart and always feel more comfortable on my feet than when working with vehicles, I ensure that the basic security procedures are never overlooked. I also understand as an old Bedouin proverb puts it *"At the narrow passage, there is no brother and no friend."*

Make your car harder to steal

Car crime is a major problem globally, be it valuables being stolen from cars or the cars themselves being stolen to be resold, exported or broken down and sold for parts. It is everyone's personal responsibility to do whatever they can to protect their valuables and their vehicles from criminals.

To know how to defend something you need to know how to attack it... So, I spoke with a renowned US repossession expert and bounty hunter Michelle Gomez. Ms. Gomez makes her living tracking down and repossessing high-end vehicles and assets for banks and insurance companies, she told us a few of the tricks used by experts in her industry.

When asked how a repossession agent would access someone's car Ms. Gomez gave us a few examples. "With the older vehicles there are tools and keys commercially available that can open a car door. If you have ever locked your keys in your car and called for road side assistance I expect the agent would have used a wire hook and plastic wedges to open your car door, someone skilled with the basic equipment can do this in seconds. With the newer high-end vehicles, we try to get access or a copy of the key fob and there are several ways we can do this 1. Our contacts at the dealership will provide us with a copy of the car key fob. Note: there are master keys to all cars. 2. We try to intercept the key fob, for example when the debtor hands the key to a hotel or restaurant valet. 3. Or we can use social engineering and try to get the debtor to give us access to the car, a classic is to use a female agent and get the debtor to let her drive his car, a lot of men are happy when they are trying to impress women, well their face changes when they realize their cars have just been repossessed!"

Ms. Gomez went on to say that it never ceased to surprise her how many people never locked their cars when they were parked in a garage. She said, "These days a lot of garage doors are electronically controlled, and their opening systems can be hacked, once we have access to the garage a lot of times the cars are open, which makes our work a lot easier". Ms. Gomez works in a regulated industry and must work within the law, but she went on to say "It's crazy when you look on the internet and there are videos and information telling people how they can open electronic garage doors, clone a car key fob etc. and this is publicly accessible.

A lot of the high-end criminals are using the Dark Web where everything is for sale and criminal hackers that can provide equipment and information on how to access cars remotely are available for hire. This is going to make car security a big problem in the future." To finish up we asked Ms. Gomez what one piece of equipment made her life a lot easier when trying to repo a high-end car, she stated straight away, "A GPS tracker, if we know where the car is and its movements we just wait for the right moment to gain entry and pick it up; without the GPS we have a lot of time consuming detective work to do."

One thing that became clear during my research on car crime was that a lot of car crimes happen in garages, supposedly secure areas. So, I sought the opinion of and expert on forced entries to see how easy it is to break into garages. I spoke to Allan London, a veteran fire fighter and rescue expert with over 40 years' experience who lives and works in South Florida in the US. Allan is also the author of the book "The Art of Effective Communication for the Fire Officer".

Mr. London explained fire fighters need to know how to quickly breach doors of all types as someone's life could depend on it. When asked about parking garages Mr London said "If it's not a solid door, say a metal grill you usually find on an apartment parking garage, we can usually gain access within 15 seconds. If it is a solid door then we need to cut our way in which with the tools we have can be noisy but not a problem." When asked about the gates to courtyards you find on private residences he said, "They are easy to defeat as long as we have access to the motors which are usually on the inside and next to the gates." We won't detail the techniques he shared with us but even with high-security gates professionals like Mr. London would not have much trouble getting in. He also stated, "As firefighters, we have to keep up to date on how to quickly gain egress into a building or parking garage to enable us to perform a rescue or extinguish a vehicle fire...these are items we need to regularly train for because in saving lives, seconds count". When asked if he thought the criminals knew these techniques he laughed and responded, "We learn from the criminals, they are the professionals!". So, it's clear that you need to take precautions, wherever you park your car.

The basic car security precautions should be

- Always park your car in a well-lit area that is covered by CCTV.
- Do not leave valuables in your car.

- Always lock the car doors, even if garage parked.
- Ensure the garage you're using is secure and has CCTV.
- Keep control of the car keys and fobs.
- Do not leave your car unattended with the engine running.
- Fit a car alarm.
- Fit a GPS tracking device.
- If valet parking the car, make sure your valuables are with you or locked in a secure place.
- Report to the police anyone you see acting suspiciously

In addition to these precautions there are also various devices on the market you can use to help secure your vehicle and valuables.

- **Steering wheel and paddle locks: These** can be relatively cheap and affordable and lock the steering wheel or peddles in place to deter and prevent the car being easily stolen. If the criminals, see your car is not an easy target they will move on to easier pickings!
- **Wheel clamps:** Usually employed for parking enforcement, wheel clamps can also be used to stop your car being stolen, especially if say you are travelling and leaving your car unattended for an extended period.
- **Car Safe:** Event though you should never leave valuables unattended in your car there may be times when traveling or valet parking that you may have to. There are discreet car safes that are available where you can store your valuables. We recommend car safes mainly for those moving valuables and cash between secure locations; if the car is highjacked the valuables will be hidden and secure. Hopefully the criminals will be apprehended by the police before they have time to access the safe.
- **Blinking LED light:** There are solar powered blinking blue and red lights that can be placed on the dash board of your car to give the impression the car has an alarm or security system running. This is a very affordable security option and a good criminal deterrent.
- **Car Alarm:** There are many car alarm systems on the market, but sadly people tend not to pay much attention to them in many places when the alarms go off. So, ensure if you fit an alarm system it has the loudest and most annoying alarm sound you can find!
- **GPS Trackers:** These are an essential device to fit to your car to help the police recover it quickly if it is stolen. Also, GPS trackers can be used to keep track of those that might be borrowing your car such as family members or employees. These days there are a lot of affordable tracking systems on the market which can be monitored from your smart phone.

- **Kill Switch:** The kill switches stop the car being "hotwired" by cutting off the electricity in the car. When fitted the switch usually takes the form of a small button hidden in the dash board that needs to be switched on before the engine will start.
- **Smartphone Applications:** There are numerous smart phone applications that can be used in conjunction with car security systems. Systems such as "Viper" allow the users to remotely control their car from the smart phones and receive alerts when the car doors are opened, the engine starts or when the car leaves a designated area or goes over a certain speed.
- **Video Surveillance:** Surveillance cameras are available for in car use to be able to monitor anyone who is driving the car. There are discreet Wi-Fi camera systems fitted with GPS trackers that will enable you to know where your vehicle is and what's going on inside of it!
- **Biometric Fingerprint Recognition:** Biometric car starters only allow a car to be started when a recognized finger print is scanned. I think in the future we can expect to see more use of biometrics for car security, including facial recognition.

Hopefully after reading this article you have a better idea on how to secure your vehicles and make life difficult for the criminals. Remember: it's your responsibility to take the necessary precautions to protect your valuables, the police are there to help with any problems you may have, but it's better to avoid the problems in the first place!

Route Selection, Ambushes & VCP's

Selecting good routes is extremely important part of your security planning especially in hostile areas or in times of civil unrest. In theory the best routes should allow the vehicles to travel at the maximum legal speed limit with as little congestion and as few stops as possible but in reality, this can be a difficult thing to achieve.

Firstly, you will need to select the routes available on a map and use programs like Google Earth to view photos of the intended route. In the perfect circumstances the routes selected would need to be driven at the time of day you'd be using them, so vehicle and pedestrian traffic flow could be assessed and at a quiet time, so a detailed survey of facilities and danger points can be compiled. You will need to plan several routes to and from each location and these will need to be varied as much as possible. In a high-risk environment if you use the same route time and time again you will be asking for trouble.

The routes need to be broken down into simple stages and the time it takes to complete each of these stages recorded. This is because if there is a loss of communication with your vehicle at a certain time, then your location can be estimated by those your checking in with and will help people to know if your vehicle is overdue and might need assistance.

You need to know the location of all the facilities along the routes such as the locations of hospitals, bathrooms, police stations, garages, hotels and so forth. Communications will need to be checked and all communication dead spots noted. The locations and payment methods (whether coins or cards) of all pay phones along the routes need to be noted. Emergency rendezvous points (RVs) will need to be allocated at positions along the routes in case of emergencies or separations, everyone using the routes will need to know the RV points.

Things that could considered as danger points on your routes would be anything that could slow you down or could conceal an ambush. These could include bridges, roundabouts, woodland, junctions, tunnels, culverts, narrow roads, one-way streets, areas of busy pedestrian or vehicle traffic, known criminal areas etc. Things to be especially suspicious of would include road works, lone-parked cars, pan-handlers, diversions and temporary stop signs. Now in reality if you live in a busy urban area I expect you will have to drive past most of the things listed to avoid on your daily journeys. In such environments you need to vary your routes as much as possible and take regular counter surveillance procedures. Also remember, if I know how someone has been trained I can usually predetermine the routes they will select, if I can do this so can the criminals.

Most conventionally trained security drivers are taught to take the most direct and fastest routes between locations, which are generally easy to determine. If I was a criminal targeting them I would just wait at a stop light along their route for them to show up. I am personally all in favor of using quite indirect routes which make it easy to identify if you're being followed and makes it a lot easier to change routes fluidly and unpredictably if required; this not the case on a motorway with limited exits and heavy traffic.

I am also not a big fan of GPS and I find it astonishing the number of people who blindly follow GPS directions right or wrong. GPS are an aid to navigation not a means of navigation. I have had many people go through my course who have gotten lost by relying in GPS; they were taken to the wrong locations or the locations I gave them were not in the GPS etc. You need to be able to use a map and compass and plan your routes properly, this might take you 5 minutes, which in today's world is a long time but better 5 minutes planning than a couple of hours driving around lost. Another take on GPS is that if I am a criminal who is watching you and see you're using a certain type of GPS, all I need to do is buy the same model and it will tell me the routes you're using between different locations, again no need for me to put you under surveillance.

Basic considerations for selecting routes are you must avoid routines, especially in daily journeys, keep your travel details secret, issue only rough timings in advance, use the most secure routes not the shortest, have a detailed reconnaissance done of the routes to be used, know what you're going to do in the case of a break down or a security issue and know where there are hospitals and other facilities on the route.

Reaction to Ambushes

The ambush tactic, in one form or another, has been used by hunters, criminals and military units for thousands of years. They are commonly used tactic in kidnappings, assassinations and they can involve anywhere from 2 to 200 personnel. Ambushes can occur on busy city streets or on remote country roads. When traveling in a vehicle, your best defense is speed. A trained ambusher will look for natural obstacles on a route which will force a vehicle to slow down.

In high risks areas you need to take into consideration what you are going to do if ambushed, your reaction will depend on the country you're in, the manpower and equipment you have available. A large percentage of attacks occur when targets are traveling in, approaching, or leaving their vehicles. Attacks can range from explosives being attached to a vehicle at traffic lights to full-scale military ambushes using assault rifles and light anti-tank weapons.

Your best defense against these attacks is your personal procedures of selecting safe routes and not using the same routes all the time and keeping details of your movements secret. If an ambush is properly planned, placed and the attackers know how to use their weapons there is a very good chance they will be successful, and you will take casualties to say the least.

The attackers have the element of surprise on their side and the whole attack could last less than five seconds; to survive, your reaction must be simple, aggressive and fast. Your main objective will be to get out of the attackers killing zone as quickly as possible. You must always be aware that the initial attack might have just been a diversion to direct you into the main ambush or that the attackers might have deployed cut off teams to take you out, if you escaped the killing zone.

If ambushed speed is your best defense, remember, fast moving targets are harder to shoot that slow moving or stationary targets. To avoid ambushes, use fast roads and try to avoid places where you are forced to drive slowly, this is difficult in busy urban areas. If you are ambushed with small arms, drive through it as fast as you can. If you are traveling in a convoy, it may be possible for the chase car to attack the ambush or if there is a lone shooter, run them over. What you do will depend on your manpower and firepower. If the road is blocked to the front of you by a large obstacle or vehicle and you have a clear road behind you reverse out, use simple driving techniques; don't use complicated techniques that you have seen in the movies.

If you are blocked to the front and rear, say in traffic or immobilized and taking fire, you will need to evacuate on foot. When you evacuate on foot stay low, bound from cover to cover and run as quickly as possible. Be aware that obvious escape routes might be booby-trapped and make maximum use of smoke or CS gas grenades to cover your escape.

Unarmed Reaction to Ambush

Here the guide lines for an unarmed contact drill that can be used if you encounter a manned road block and are in an area where you cannot carry weapons.

A consideration on weapons: In some hostile environments, criminals and terrorists put up roadblocks that can contain anywhere from 5 to 200 criminals or guerillas carrying automatic weapons. Think about it, you may have a couple of 9mm pistols in your vehicle but 5 guys with AK-47's can put out 150 rounds, which will go through un-armored cars in just a few seconds. Additionally, in some places, if you are a foreigner and you are caught with a pistol by criminals or terrorists, you could be mistaken for being a spy and executed on the spot. If you are going to carry a pistol, it's best to go with a type not issued to law enforcement and military personnel; a Nickel plated .38 revolver says your carful where as a Glock can say your police!

This drill was worked out for a client who lived on a very volatile Caribbean island. Firearms were available but if they were found by local police at a routine road block they could lead to the client being arrested or getting severe beating. The client's main threat was from driving into illegal roadblocks at night. This is a simplified version of what I worked out for him.

- The client fitted high power spotlights to his vehicle. If he drove into a roadblock at night, he would hit the spotlights for a few seconds and temporally blind and surprise the criminals.
- At the same time, he would reverse away from the roadblock. The client always traveled with another person at night whose job it was to drop smoke dischargers on the road to cover them as they reversed away.
- Whenever possible and safe to do so, the client would turn the vehicle around get out of the area as quickly as possible. If chased by criminals, the client's car was modified, so all the rear lights could be extinguished, and he could drive with only the front parking lights on. In the vehicle, there was a high-powered hand-held spotlight, which the passenger was to shine into the face of the driver of the chasing car, to blind them and hopefully cause them to crash.

This drill is simple, but it still took a fair bit of organizing and practice to get right. You need to work out what threats that you're most likely to encounter, then plan your reaction and then practice it.

Vehicle security considerations

Wherever you are working or living at some point you will have to use vehicles, for most people they are part of their everyday lives. Driving its self can be a dangerous task in many places and as we have seen many kidnappings, robberies and assassinations occur when people are in or around their vehicles.

Vehicles should be regarded as an important piece of your equipment and should be well maintained and never treated as a toy. Before you take a vehicle out basic maintenance checks need to be done, like checking the battery, oil, fuel level, tires, water, spare tire, break down and emergency kit. You should always ensure you have a good means of communications and that you regularly check in with trusted people who can send assistance in the case of an emergency. You should also always know the routes you are driving and the location of any facilities along those routes that could be of use to you whether it's a coffee shop with a bathroom or a hospital with an emergency room.

Chauffer's & Drivers

If you are traveling to another country it might make sense to hire a chauffeur, driver or bodyguard. Over the years I have encounter people who claim to experienced chauffeurs, drivers and bodyguards but in reality, were a liability. The main thing you need to consider when hiring drivers or security personnel is whether they can be trusted. You may be paying them several hundred dollars a day but are they going to be loyal to you if they are offered a percentage of your ransom or their families are threatened. This is where you need to be personally security aware and know where you're going and what you're doing, never unconditionally trust anyone with your life or to have your best interests at heart.

If you are using a driver you should check his qualifications and make sure he can actually drive to a good standard and the vehicle you're using is well maintained. You want drivers and bodyguards who are in good physical health and who don't not drink too much or take any drugs. It is impractical for someone to be both bodyguard and driver; drivers must concentrate on driving their vehicles safely and must stay with the vehicle always. If you are in an area where there is an active threat, you should hire additional trained and trusted bodyguards. The quality of bodyguards and trained security drivers can vary greatly and in most places the standards are low. I have seen many clients over the years being driven around protected by guys who just happen to firearms permits or are moonlighting local police who for all these clients know are working for the criminals also.

Several years ago, I went with two American clients to an island in the Caribbean where the crime and kidnapping rates are high by most standards. My clients were dealing with a European company on the island that were to provide them with security, but they want me to go along as they were not getting a positive feeling from this company. So, I arrange extra trusted local armed security personnel and an armored vehicle to accompany us.

The population of the island is predominantly of African descent, so my clients and I had no real chance of blending in. My business partner met us with our local security guys inside of the airport, as there is always a high risk when leaving airports because you are being channeled. We then went to look for the security personnel who had come to pick up my clients from the European company they were dealing with. The European bodyguard was easy to spot as he was the only white guy outside of the airport holding a sign with mine and my client's names on. At this stage the bodyguard did not know I was providing security for my clients, as we going to his vehicle I informed him that I had my own local security personnel who would be following us back to our hotel. As we drove through the city my guys in a black SUV drove very aggressively and stayed close to our vehicle. When we got to our hotel the European bodyguard told us to stay in the car as he thought we were being followed and was going to check the car out behind us; we were being followed, by my security people, he had not been listening when I informed him of this.

This bodyguard who I know must have done at least five years' European military service and I expect at least one specialist training course made two very big mistakes that could have led to serious problems. One, he stood out at the airport and by having mine and my client's full names on a piece of paper was letting everyone know who we were. If a criminal with an internet capable cell phone had Googled my client's names they would have seen, they were worth kidnapping. Two, why did he wait until we got back to our hotel to check out my security guy's car that was following us. If he thought they were a threat he should have asked us if we knew them, taken evasive action or stayed mobile and called for support; which this European company claimed to have on standby. If my guys had been criminals, this bodyguard had just taken them to our place of residence. I still don't know what he was going to achieve by going and checking my guys out at the hotel as he had no authority to stop and question anyone, he was also carrying a firearm which he could not legally have a permit to carry.

This is a good example of supposedly trained security personnel not knowing or caring about what they are doing. I expect they had not had any problems or though no one would target them and had relaxed to a point of being ineffective, this happens if security personnel are not well managed. The other funny thing was as we were leaving our hotel to go to my client's first meeting with the European company the car they supplied got a flat tire and it had no break down kit. So, we transferred everyone to my local guy's vehicle and left the driver to deal with the flat. We let the European bodyguard sit in the front as we felt sorry for him; he was not having a good day!

If you are going to use local drivers and security personnel try to get them some training or at least go through your basic emergency plans with them. If you are under a threat, let them know that the threat also applies to them and their families. Make sure they take the relevant security measures and are always vigilant for the threat of criminal surveillance. Your driver should never stand outside the vehicle when you approach it, have a safety signal with them and do not approach the vehicle until they give the signal. The driver should always be behind the wheel with the engine running and ready to make a quick escape in the case of an emergency. On arrival at your destination the driver should remain behind the wheel of the vehicle; it would be the job of the bodyguard to open your door, if required. You should always know where the driver is and how to contact them. If the driver is not 100% trusted only inform them of routes or destinations just before or after the journey has started and do not give them any long-term schedules.

Basic vehicle security considerations

Vehicles need to be secured or manned always, if they are left unattended, they, and the area around them, must be searched for IEDs, electronic surveillance devices, contraband and anything suspicious. The area around a vehicle must be searched as you approach it for any suspicious vehicles or people; the criminals may have found your car and are waiting for your approach it to kidnap or assassinate you. I always try to park my car as far away from others as possible, that way there is no cover for anyone to hide and if any other car is parked close to mine they are immediately suspicious.

If you keep the vehicle in a locked garage still always lock doors and trunk, you will also need to search the exterior of the garage for IEDs, electronic surveillance devices and signs of forced entry. If the vehicle cannot be garaged try to park it in a secure, guarded area or somewhere that is covered by surveillance cameras. Driveways and regularly used routes from your residence to main roads should regularly be search for IEDs and signs of criminal activity. A vehicle needs to be searched after being serviced or repaired and after being left unattended for any length of time, here are some guidelines on how to search a vehicle:

- Always search the general area around a vehicle for any explosive devices or suspicious people waiting to ambush you. Always check the outside of a garage for any signs of a force entry before you go in and check garage doors and drive ways for signs of booby traps, land mines and ambushes.
- Turn off all radios and cell phones and check the immediate area surrounding the car for disturbances, wires, oil/fluid stains, footprints, etc. It helps to keep vehicles a little dirty as you will be able to see smears in the dirt if someone was trying to break in.
- Visual check through the windows for anything thing out of place or wires, etc.
- Get down on your hands and knees and check underneath the vehicle, inside fenders, wheels and arches for any devices. Also check for cut tires, lose wheel nuts and devices placed under the wheels. This is where a flashlight and a search mirror can come in handy.
- Check the exhaust as it is a very easy place to put an improvised explosive device. You can have bolts or wire mesh put in to exhausts to stop IEDs from being placed in them; if you do this, make sure the bolts or wire mess is not visible as this can draw attention to the car.
- Slowly open the car doors and check the Interior of the vehicle even if there is no signs of a forced entry. Do the same for the trunk and make sure to search the spare tire and break down kit.
- Open the hood slowly and check the engine. Again, it might be helpful to keep the engine dirty as new wires and hand prints are easy to see.
- Final turn on the engine and check all the electrics.

This is just a guide to searching vehicles but as you can see to do a thorough search can take time and would require someone to be watching the back of the searcher. Your best defense is to deny the criminal access to your vehicle, but this can prove to be very difficult in the real world.

Vehicle drills

If you drive yourself consider undertaking some advanced driving training, I see little need for evasive driver training but can see applications for people to learn to be able to handle vehicles at speed and in hazardous weather. Again, vehicle drills cannot be learnt from manuals or videos, you will need to learn them from an experienced advanced trained driver. Always check out the instructor's background, qualifications and reputation, look for those that offer sensible driving courses and not wannabe spy holidays.

The main thing you need to learn is how to drive safely and to be able to identify any possible threats and avoid them. In most large towns and cities, you will not be able to perform such things as J turns or other evasive maneuvers due to lack of space and traffic, so you must always be aware of what is going on around you. The main thing I tell people is to keep as much space as possible between you and the car in front as this can give you some space to maneuver in congested traffic.

When you watch the movies and there is a car chase and the cars are skidding all over the place check the state of the roads they are on. Chances are the roads will be wet, and the tires on the cars will have minimal tread. This is the same on most evasive driving courses, but these are also usually done on private roads or open areas where there is no other traffic. Think about why you put decent tires on your vehicles; to stop them from skidding and spinning out of control right? When you are driving around you always want to be thinking of where you could take evasive action, in urban areas there will be few places where you could spin your car around and drive against the traffic flow; that's Hollywood.

If the criminals or terrorists are in anyway professional they will attack you when your car is penned in and you cannot take any evasive maneuvers, not on wide open roads. It's a common street kid tactics in a lot of Latin American cities to rob cars at traffic lights that are at least two cars back from the stop light with other cars behind them; these cars are stuck and cannot escape. If street kids on bicycles with at most a rusty revolver have worked out how to jack people in cars don't you think their big bothers have also?

Security considerations for using vehicles

- Always check the area around the vehicle before you approach it.
- Search the vehicle prior to use for IEDs, electronic surveillance devices and contraband.
- Whenever possible, use a trained and trusted driver.
- Always keep a spare set of keys for the vehicle on you in case the driver loses his or is taken out by the criminals.

- Be aware of the vehicle's capabilities; make sure the driver has experience driving that type of vehicle.
- Always drive safely at the maximum, safest speed, within the legal speed limit.
- Always carry out basic maintenance checks, before you go anywhere and check that communications work before leaving a safe area.
- Make sure you know what to do if your car breaks down; will someone come to get you, or will you call for roadside assistance?
- In rural areas things that should be included in your break down kit should include cans of fix-a-flat, air compressor, jump leads, tire plugging kit, tube to siphon gas, gas cans and a tow rope.
- Know which routes your taking and keep maps in the vehicle for all areas you're traveling in. Also have alternative routes prepared that have been driven and checked out.
- Inform the security personnel or advance security at a location 10 to 15 minutes, before your arrival.
- Constantly check behind you for criminal surveillance vehicles and be suspicious of motorbikes, especially with two people on them.
- When being followed by a motorbike always watch to see if both the rider's hands are on the handle bars, if you only see one hand, what is the other holding or doing?
- Make full use of your mirrors; put a mirror on the passenger side for the bodyguard to use.
- Regularly carry out counter-surveillance drills and always be watching for any cars following you or suspicious people along regularly used routes.
- Keep a good distance from the car in front, so you can drive around it in an emergency and try to avoid being blocked by other vehicles.
- Never let the vehicle fuel tank to go below half full and know where all gas stations are along your route.
- Keep doors locked when traveling between locations and do not open windows or sunroof more than an inch, so things cannot be thrown in.
- Always be prepared to take evasive action, be aware of danger points on your routes and drive towards the center of the road to have space for evasive maneuvers.
- Blend in with your environment; don't drive expensive cars in poor areas, etc.
- Be suspicious of all roadblocks, temporary stop signs and car accidents, etc. Never stop to pick up hitchhikers or help other motorists, as these could be covers for an ambush or carjacking.

- Keep vehicle keys secure and know who has all the spare keys and access to the vehicle.
- Remember others can monitor tracking devices and help services such as OnStar, then get the details of where you are and your routine without the need for surveillance.
- Be extra vigilant at traffic lights and in slow moving traffic.
- Keep the vehicle in a locked garage when not in use and lock all doors and the trunk.
- Wherever legal reverse park; this will help if fast get away is required.
- Stop vehicles as close to the entrances and exits as possible, this limits your exposure time on the street.
- Always use seat belts, especially when driving at speed or taking evasive action, also keep a safety knife handy to cut away seat belts and break windows in the case of a crash.
- Driver must stay with the vehicle and behind wheel unless told otherwise, bodyguard always opens client's door not the driver.

Car bags

When working with a vehicle, it makes sense to keep all your important and essential equipment in a car bag; this can be a hold-all or day-sack. You do not want to leave your equipment in an unattended vehicle; if the vehicle is stolen, you lose your kit, which could be embarrassing, especially where weapons and confidential information is concerned. From a tactical point of view, if you are in an ambush or contact and must evacuate on foot, you will want to have any confidential information and emergency equipment with you.

What you carry in the car bag will vary greatly depending where you are and what you are doing. For example, what you need in an urban environment will be different from what you could need in a very rural environment. What I have listed here is just a guide to what you may need; you need to keep things real and not include "what if" kit that you will never use, remember if things go wrong and you must run you don't want a bag weighing 100 lbs on your back.

Car bag equipment: Basic

- A decent bag that is easy to carry, preferably a day sack or something that can be carried on you back, so your hands are left free.
- All equipment should be in individual water proof bags or containers. This is to keep everything dry, organized and clean.
- Good maps and street plans of the area your traveling through and a compass.

- Any confidential information such as orders, codes, designated routes, operational procedures etc.
- Radio and communications equipment, chargers and spare batteries.
- A good first aid kit.
- A good flash light and spare batteries.
- A bag of coins for parking meters and pay phones.
- A camera, for taking photos of anything suspicious or things you think need recording.
- Water proofed note pad and a selection of pens.

Car bag equipment: Potential threat environment

- Radio scanners can be used to scan the emergency services radio frequencies, and this can provide you with an early warning of potential problems or criminal and terrorist incidents in your area. In some areas, there are restrictions on the use of scanners– always check.
- Spotlights can be used at night to shine in the face and blind the drive of a threat vehicle, which is following or chasing you.
- Smoke dischargers, military style smoke grenades are illegal to possess in most places. What are legal, though, are the smoke distress signals that are carried on yachts and maritime vessels. These can be bought at most boat shops and are not that expensive, they usually can discharge about a minuets worth of red smoke. Smoke can be used to provide cover from view if you are ambushed or need to evacuate on foot. In addition, it can be used to cause a distraction in say an urban environment, so you can evacuate the area.
- Weapons– in some areas you cannot carry weapons on your person but can carry them in a secure case; the case can go in your bag. Where there may be a need for a long gun, such as a shotgun or assault rifle, and these cannot be carried openly, they can go into a car bag.

Food and drink

Depending on where you are and the length of your journey, you may want to carry some form of food and drink with you.

- Drink: It's always handy to have a thermos flask of coffee or tea available, for morale reasons, if nothing else. With drinks and liquids, you must insure they do not spill or leak over documents and equipment. Highly caffeinated and sugary coffee or sports drinks can be included in your car bag for emergencies, as these can give you an energy boost, when you need it and can help you to stay awake when you're tired.

- Food: If you are carrying food as with liquids you need to insure they do not spill or leak over documents and equipment. If you take a sandwich or other perishable food with you make sure you do not leave them in the car bag for any extended length of time and they go bad. It is also good protocol, if sharing a vehicle with others, not to carry strong smelling food; it might not smell good to everyone. Emergency foods that can be carried include chocolate bars, nuts, raisins, etc. These will give you energy, are compact and have a long shelf life.

Remember: If you use any emergency supplies, replace them!

Car bag equipment: Rural environment

If you are traveling in rural areas, the equipment you carry in your car bag will differ from that of someone who operates in a urban area. It would make sense to carry in the trunk of your vehicle with your break down kit some flash lights, blankets, water, a small camping stove, tea or coffee kit and some tinned food, in case you break down and no one can get to you for a long period of time. This equipment can fit into a plastic storage box.

The equipment you carry in your car bag will depend on how far, or how long you will have to travel, and what type of terrain you will have to cross to get to a safe area, if you have to evacuate on foot and leave your vehicle. You would have worked this out as part of your route selection.

- Sensible shoes; you or your group members may have just left an urban business or social function type of environment and still be wearing city shoes or high heels; these are not the best things to run cross country in. Carry some light sensible shoes that can be put on when a safe distance from the vehicle in the case of an ambush, etc.
- Waterproof clothes and shelter: The best piece of equipment that can protect you from the rain and wind while moving and provide a shelter while laid up is a military type poncho. These are also compact.
- Fire-starting equipment or a compact camp stove. If it will take you 24 hours or more to get to a safe area, it could make sense to be able to make a fire to keep warm, heat food or brew hot drinks.
- Food and drink: If you are likely to have to travel on foot for an extended period of time, you will need enough food and drink to provide you with energy for the journey. This could be tinned foods or, where water is freely available, dried foods. You also want to include packages of instant tea,

coffee or chocolate drinks. Not only will hot food and drinks give you energy, it is also an excellent morale lifter.

- Water carriers and cooking utensils: Depending where you are will depend on how much water you will need to carry. If there are plenty of fresh water streams, etc., in your area, you will not have to carry as much as you would, if you were in a desert type area. There are many different types of water bottles on the market; consider using a thermos flask or two, as you can keep them full of hot drinks, for when you are on the move. The best item to carry for boiling water or cooking in is a metal military mug; these are compact but be careful not to burn your lips when drinking from them; you can cover the rim with gaffer tape to prevent burning your lips. You will also need a plastic spoon and a pocketknife with a tin opener on it, if you are carrying tinned foods.
- Equipment for hot climates, if you're operating in a hot climate, things to carry in your car bag could include extra water, sun block, insect repellant, wide brim hat, sun glasses, etc.
- Equipment for cold climates: If you're operating in a cold climate, additional things to carry in your car bag could include warm clothing including hat and gloves, light sleeping bag, etc.

This is only a guide to what you may want to carry with you. We are not going to get into wilderness survival and navigation techniques, as that is another subject, of which, if you're operating in rural areas, you should have at least a basic knowledge.

Orlando Wilson

Orlando's experience in risk management business started in 1988 when he enlisted in the British Army and volunteered for a 22-month operational tour in Northern Ireland in an infantry unit. This tour of duty gave him among other things an excellent grounding in anti-terrorist operations. He then joined his unit's Reconnaissance Platoon where he undertook intensive training in small-unit warfare and also undertook training with specialist units such as the RM Mountain and Arctic Warfare Cadre and US Army's Special Forces.

Since leaving the British army in 1993 he has initiated, provided and managed an extensive range of specialist security, investigation and tactical training services to international corporate, private and government clients. Some services of which, have been the first of their kind in the respective countries.

His experience has included providing close protection for Middle Eastern Royal families and varied corporate clients, specialist security and asset protection, diplomatic building and embassy security, kidnap and ransom services, corporate investigations and intelligence, para-military training for private individuals and specialist tactical police units and government agencies. Over the years, he has become accustomed to the types of complications that can occur, when dealing with international law enforcement agencies and the problem of organized crime.

Orlando is the chief consultant for Risks Incorporated and is also a published author and has been interviewed and written articles for numerous media outlets ranging from the New York Times to Soldier of Fortune Magazine on topics ranging from kidnapping, organized crime, surveillance to maritime piracy.

Printed in France by Amazon
Brétigny-sur-Orge, FR

15996668R00036